Well-known tales from

PANCHATANTRA

Om
KIDZ

An imprint of Om Books International

Reprinted in 2017

An imprint of Om Books International

Corporate & Editorial Office
A 12, Sector 64, Noida 201 301
Uttar Pradesh, India
Phone: +91 120 477 4100
Email: editorial@ombooks.com
Website: www.ombooksinternational.com

Sales Office
107, Ansari Road, Darya Ganj, New Delhi 110 002, India
Phone: +91 11 4000 9000
Fax: +91 11 2327 8091
Email: sales@ombooks.com
Website: www.ombooks.com

ISBN: 978-81-87107-87-3

Printed in India

10 9 8 7

Contents

The Intelligent Hare

Once upon a time, there was a dense forest, which had lots of animals and birds living in it. All the animals and birds lived together happily. No animal or bird ever killed a smaller one for food. However, there was one exception,

and that was the king of the jungle – an evil lion. The lion hunted around the forest at all times and killed the animals for food.

One day, the animals could not take it anymore. So they got together for a meeting. "It is not fair," said the bear. "He is killing so many of us, that one day this forest will not have any animals left."

So, all the animals, led by the elephant decided to talk to the king. "Your majesty," said the elephant, "You are killing so many of us, when you need only one for food!"

"We suggest you kill only one of us each day," said the clever fox.

The lion thought for a few minutes and said, "Fine! One of you will come to me each day

as food. The day you do not turn up, I will kill all of you." The animals agreed.

From that day, one animal would leave his family to go to the lion as food. This went on for many days, till one morning it was the hare's turn to go to the king. The intelligent hare was walking to the lion's den, when he saw a well on the way. Suddenly, a bright thought struck him, and he almost ran to the den.

Seeing him, the lion roared and said, "I was wondering where you were!" The hare replied, "Master, I was on my way to your den. But on my way, I was stopped by another lion who said he was the king of the jungle. He called you a cheat and wanted you to fight him to prove your supremacy."

The lion was livid with rage. He said, "Bring him here and I will teach him a lesson." But the hare managed to persuade the lion to go with him. He guided the lion to the well and asked him to look inside.

The foolish lion looked at his own reflection in the water and thinking it was his competitor, jumped inside. That was his end. All the animals rejoiced at the intelligence of the clever hare.

The Four Friends

In a forest lived three friends – turtle, crow and a little mouse. All day long, the friends would eat and play together. One day, while the friends were sitting near the lake, they saw a deer running for life.

Soon he came near the place where they were sitting, and fell down on the mud. He had fainted. The turtle sprinkled some water from the lake on him. In a

few minutes, the deer opened his eyes.
He told the three friends that he was
running for life from a hunter.

The crow flew right to the top of a
large tree to check where the hunter

was. He came down and assured the deer that the hunter had caught some other animal, and was going back home.

From that day on, the deer joined the group of friends. Together, they lived happily, until one day the deer did not reach the usual place where the friends would meet.

The crow was worried and flew through the forest looking for him. He found the deer caught in a hunter's net. He flew right back

to where his friends were waiting, and told the mouse what had happened. The mouse scurried across the forest and found the deer. Slowly and steadily he cut through the net. Meanwhile, the animals saw the turtle walking towards them. The deer thought to

himself, "What lovely friends I have! All of them have come to help me in my time of need." Just when the deer was thinking about his friends, the crow alerted everyone about the hunter approaching. The mouse quickly

scurried into a hole. The crow was perched on top of a tree, and the deer got up and sprinted away. Finally, only the poor turtle was left behind.

The hunter picked up the turtle, strung him on his bow and walked away. A few minutes after the hunter had left the spot, the three friends got together and worked out a plan.

The hunter was walking along the lake, when he saw a dead deer lying on the path.

He put the turtle down, thinking it was his lucky day and walked across to the deer. When he was nearing the deer, the crow cawed and to the hunter's surprise, the deer got up and sprinted away.

The hunter could not believe his eyes. He turned around, and saw that the turtle he had tied to his bow was no longer there. The mouse had cut the strings while the hunter

had gone towards the deer and the turtle had slipped into the lake.

The poor hunter was left crying on the path with no catch, while the good friends happily thanked each other.

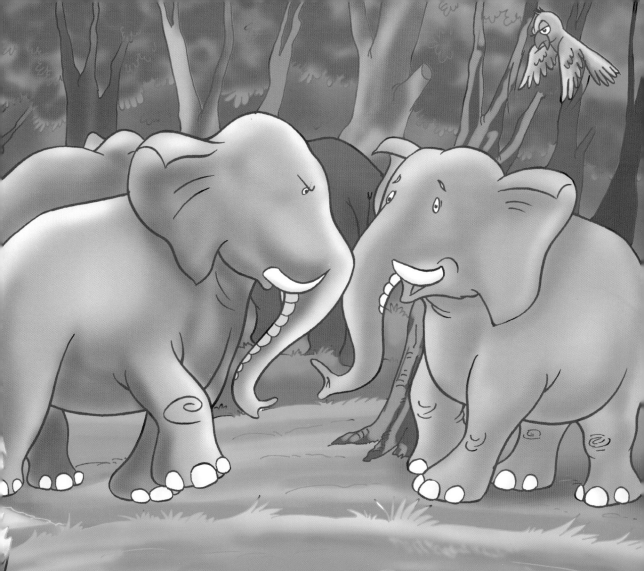

The Hare and the
Elephant King

Long, long ago, the elephants ruled the jungle instead of the lion. They were big, strong and the mightiest of all.

Unfortunately, one hot summer, the water in the forest dried up. The animals started dying one by one. The elephant king was worried. He had to save the animals. He had heard about

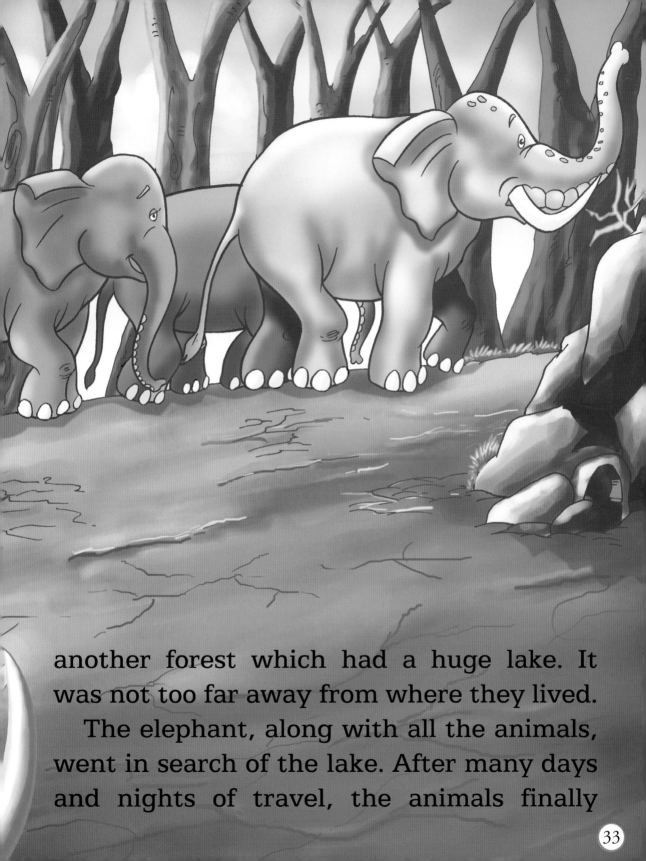

another forest which had a huge lake. It was not too far away from where they lived. The elephant, along with all the animals, went in search of the lake. After many days and nights of travel, the animals finally found the lake. They were full of joy seeing water after so many days, and rushed into the lake. Then they decided that they would come to the lake every day.

But, in their joy, they did not see that they were trampling across a colony of hares, which was living in that forest for ages. The hares were getting hurt. The trampling of the animals was happening every day.

So, one day, after the animals had left the lake, the hares got together to work out a plan, to save their lives. Their leader was sent to the elephant king to discuss the matter with him.

The hare told the elephant king, "Your majesty! I come from the land of the moon, who is our king. He is the owner of the lake and forbids you or your subjects to drink from it. So

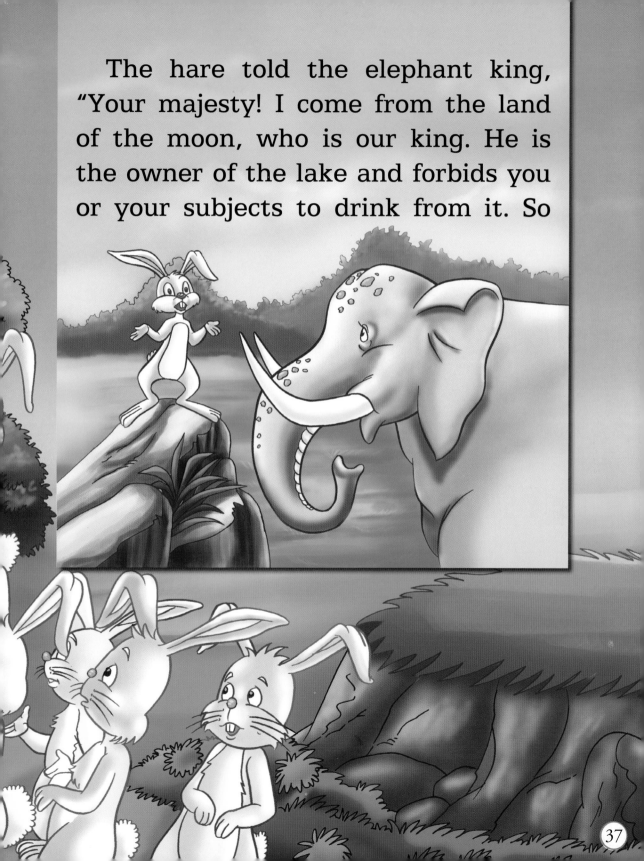

I request you to find another lake." The elephant replied, "Take me to your king. I would like to meet him." The clever hare took the elephant to the lake during the night and pointed to the reflection of the shining moon in the water.

He said, "Look how our king is shaking with anger at you!" The elephant saw the moon shivering in the water, and assumed that what the hare was saying was true.

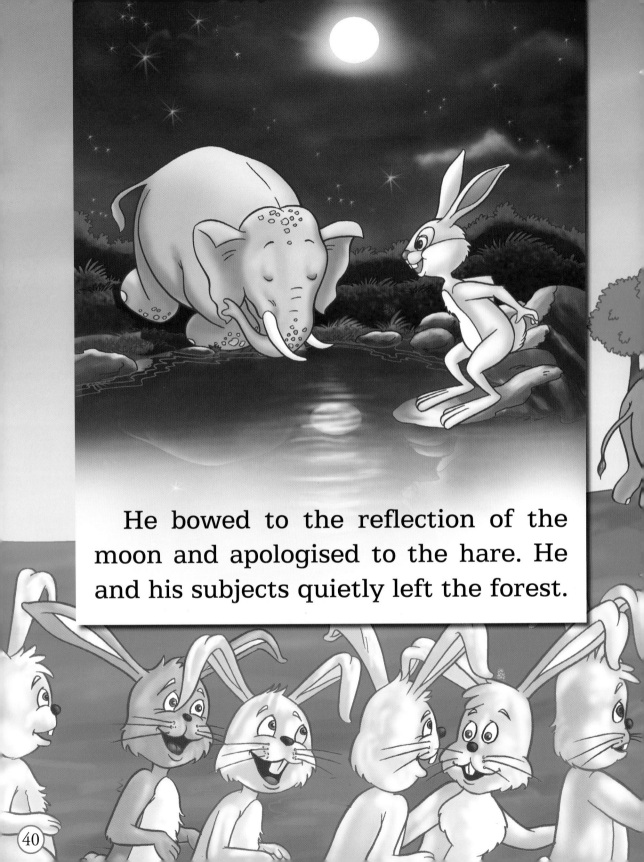

He bowed to the reflection of the moon and apologised to the hare. He and his subjects quietly left the forest.

The animals never returned to the lake.
Thus, the hare saved his entire colony with
his bravery and quick thinking.

The Jackal's Quick Thinking

One day, a jackal found a dead elephant and was very happy that he had found food for many days.

But unfortunately, the elephant's hide was too thick to bite into. The jackal was wondering what he would do, when he saw a lion approaching.

He saluted the lion and said, "Oh great king! This humble gift lying in front of you is my offering to you." The lion replied, "I do not take what is killed by others. So consider this as my gift to you."

Saying so, the lion walked away. A few
minutes later, a tiger crossed the same path.
The jackal knew that he would have to use
some quick thinking. So he said, "My lord!
Please pass by quickly. I am guarding this

elephant, which was killed by the mighty lion himself. The lion has vowed to kill any tiger that he sees; as a tiger had once tried to eat an elephant that the lion had killed. So your life is in grave danger!" The tiger thanked the jackal for warning him and ran for his life.

Just when the jackal was getting impatient about finding someone to bite into the elephant's hide, he saw a leopard. He knew he could use the leopard's sharp teeth to solve his problem. So he told the leopard, "Oh great

leopard! I am guarding the elephant, while the lion who killed it, has gone for a bath. Please feast yourself on it before he returns."

The leopard replied, "I would be mad to do that, for the lion would kill me!" To that the

cunning jackal said, "Do not worry! You can feast on it till he returns. I will signal you when I see him coming." The jackal waited for the leopard to bite into the hide and then signalled the lion's arrival. The leopard ran away in fear.

The jackal sat down to enjoy his catch when he spotted another hungry jackal coming his way. Without wasting any time, he jumped on to that jackal, and beat him to a pulp in a bitter fight.

Finally, the victorious jackal sat down to enjoy the feast he had worked so hard for!

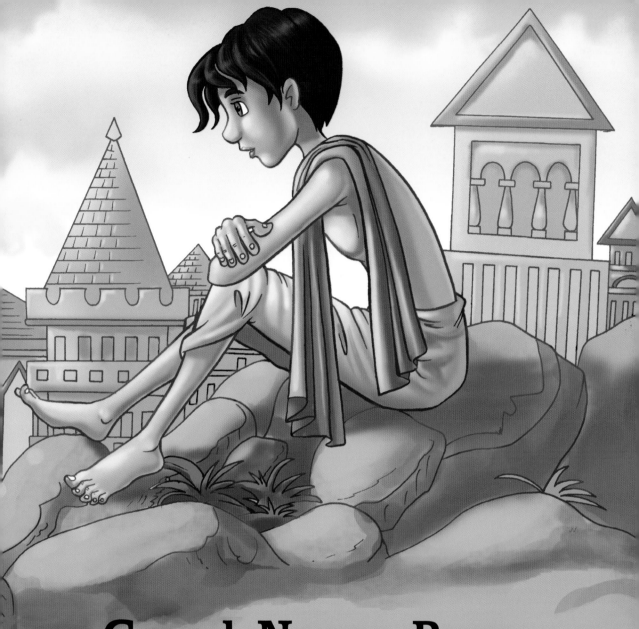

Greed Never Pays

In a small town, lived four young boys. They were so poor that they decided to leave their town and travel to earn money.

They took a dip in a river nearby and when they came out of the water after offering their prayers, a sage greeted them. The boys narrated their suffering to the sage, who took

pity on them and gave them four pearls. He told them, "I am giving you four pearls – one for each one of you. Travel to the mountains and stop when a pearl slips from your hand. You are sure to find a treasure there."

The boys left for the mountains in search for treasure. They were just a quarter way up the mountain range, when a pearl slipped out of a boy's hand. All of them stopped, and dug up the spot excitedly. They found copper at the end of their digging. The boy was very happy and decided to go back home with copper. But the other three felt that they needed to find gold.

They travelled for a few more days, when a pearl slipped out of another boy's hand. On digging up the place, they found silver. The

boy decided to pack the silver and head for his little town, while the other two decided to travel ahead in their search for gold.

They travelled across rough mountains, when another pearl slipped and fell at a spot. The boys dug up the spot and finally, there it was ... shining gold!

One of the two boys said, "Look! We have finally found what we were looking for. Let us take it and go home." To that, the other boy replied, "Think about it, every step we

have taken ahead has given better results – first it was copper, then it was silver and now it is gold. I am sure there must be something more precious than gold ahead."

Saying so, the boy decided to go ahead, while the one who found gold, could only shake his head in disapproval at his friend's greed.

So three boys had gone home with their treasures, and the fourth boy travelled for

days and finally, he came across a spot where there was a man standing with a wheel spinning on top of his head. The boy asked, "Who are you and why is this wheel spinning on your head?"

The moment the boy uttered these words, the wheel shifted from the man's head to the boy's head. The wheel caused a lot of pain, and the boy looked at the man in disbelief and cried, "Take this thing off my head!"

The man replied, "No one can remove the wheel. You will be saved from this pain when another boy like you comes to this spot in search of wealth and asks the same question you just asked. The magic of this wheel is that

you will not feel any hunger or thirst. But you will only feel the pain that greed causes."

The man left, while the boy stood there repenting at how his greed had brought him such misfortune.

The Crane and the Crab

Once upon a time, in a lake lived an old crane. He was so old that it was becoming very difficult for him to hunt for food. One day, he was standing on a rock crying, when a crab came to him and asked, "Uncle, what has made you so unhappy?"

The smart crane realised the opportunity. He replied, "I now repent for my sins of eating the fish in this lake during all these years."

The crab was surprised. He asked, "What makes you think like this?"

The crane replied, "I have heard that a dark future awaits these fish. It is said that there will be no rain in the coming years and the lake will dry up. So, all the fish you are seeing today will die one by one. Soon there will be none left in the lake."

The crab asked the crane for a solution and sure enough, the crane offered to help the fish by carrying them one by one to a bigger lake. Just as the crane had expected, the crab went and talked to all the fish. The innocent fish trusted the crane, who carried one fish every day in his beak. He would go a distance

and then smash the unsuspecting fish against a rock, kill it and eat it.

For days, the crane feasted on one fish after the other, until it was the crab's turn. The crab had been waiting for his chance with great excitement.

He told the crane, "Uncle, it is finally my turn to go and swim in the water of the new lake."

The crane carried the crab on his back and flew the distance he always did. Suddenly the crab saw piles of

fish bones lying at a distance. He quickly realised what the crane had been doing for so long. He asked the crane, "Uncle, why do I see so many bones lying around?" The crane replied, "You have been foolish to trust me. Now you will die the same way as your fish friends did."

The crab was quick to answer. He asked, "Is it?" And before the crane could react, he had bitten the crane's neck to death.

He then took the neck back to the lake where the other fish were waiting for the crane to come back and take them. He told the fish, "From now on, we have learnt not to trust anyone so quickly."

The remaining fish rejoiced at the crab's quick thinking, which had saved their lives.